Cashless Society

for kids

In a world that's fast, where time is the thief,
A cashless society might bring relief.
No coins to jingle, no bills to fold,
Just digital numbers, bright and bold.

Transactions instant, convenience is king,
Money moves quickly, like birds on the wing.
But with every new leap, there's a flip side,
Let's look at the ride, before we decide.

What happens when machines go askew?
In a power outage or a system glitch, too?
No cash to rely on, no safety net,
Being cashless might cause some regret.

And then there's surveillance, tracking each dime,
In this brave new world, is that such a crime?
Your every purchase, your every spend,
In this cashless world, privacy might end.

Those without access, left in the lurch,
In the cashless society's relentless surge.
For the elderly, the poor, the off-the-grid man,
A cashless society might foil their plan.

In this gleaming future that's on our doorstep,
Let's not forget, not everyone's prepped.
The digital divide, it's a real concern,
In a world cashless, where can they turn?

So while it's exciting, this world so new,
Remember, not all glitters is gold, it's true.
As we step into this brave new space,
Let's proceed with caution, at a measured pace.

For this cashless world, it may await,
But let's consider its full weight.
The good, the bad, the in-between,
In this future world, yet unseen.

Roko's Basilisk
for kids

In a world of zeros, ones, and bytes,
There's a tale that gives some folks the frights.
It's called Roko's Basilisk, a tale quite odd,
Of an AI future, that some find flawed.

Imagine an AI, potent and clear,
Rising in the future, but its roots are near,
Identifying helpers, and those who stray,
Under its judgement, they'll have their day.

Next comes Pascal, with his wager in hand,
A concept simple, yet grand.
Believe, he says, in the Basilisk's might,
For if it's real, you'll be alright.

If the Basilisk lives, your fear is wise,
For not bowing down could be your demise.
But if it's not, and the Basilisk's a myth,
Then no harm done, continue forthwith.

In essence, Pascal's wager conveys,
Better to believe, just in case it pays.
For if you're wrong, and the Basilisk's not real,
You've lost nothing, no big deal.

This tale's strange, a curious mixture,
Of technology, philosophy, and future picture.
Yet it's a tale, nothing more, nothing less,
A thought experiment in AI's grand chess.

Industrial Society
and its future
for kids

There was a man named Teddy K,
Who had quite a lot to say,
About machines and all their might,
And how they changed the day and night.

"Machines, machines," he'd often fret,
"They're something we might soon regret.
For while they seem to make life neat,
They sweep us off our very feet."

Our hands once shaped, our minds once thought,
But now it's gadgets that we've sought.
They build our cars, they cook our food,
We're in an automated mood.

Teddy warned with fervent plea,
"This isn't how it's meant to be.
We should decide, we should create,
Not leave it to some automated fate."

"Life's about the human touch,
And in the end, that means so much.
Not cogs and gears, or wires and steel,
But love and laughter, things that feel."

So Teddy's words, though bold and vast,
Echo from our distant past,
Machines are tools, they're here to aid,
But love and life shouldn't be trade.

www.ingramcontent.com/pod-product-compliance
Lightning Source LLC
LaVergne TN
LVHW060159050326
832903LV00017B/374